Magitar

An Adventurous Introduction to Guitar Technique

Book 1: The Foundation

Introduction

As a young teenager, I used to love role playing games. Not the pen and paper ones, but the massive online ones. For those who do not know what those are, you can think of them as giant virtual worlds with built in point systems.

These point systems kept people glued to their screen for hours and days, obsessing over obtaining the next level. The points awarded dictated everything from your special powers, to where you could travel. It was quite a lot of fun.

People would stay up for hours, and obsess over gaining more experience points. More attribute points. All night, drinking coffee and typing away with virtual friends they had never met, but knew intimately. Though fun, the drawback was that few real skills are derived from this past time.

If only I had that kind of dedication to just guitar at that age. :)

As a teacher, I have often through to myself: "How can I create the same type of experience for guitar?" Now, not everyone thinks that grinding exercises for the guitar are boring. I personally love them, and benefit from the daily. But for some, it just is not interesting.

That is very unfortunate, because your warmup exercises are the most important part of your technical progression with the guitar. You have to be able to touch the guitar correctly in order to play it fluently. You also have to be able to measure how good you currently are, so that you can set yourself upon a path of progress.

It also helps not to have 1,000 different exercises. Many guitar books take this erroneous path: The more exercises, the better. Now, I will admit that approach works for sight reading. But not necessarily technique.

In Ricardo Iznaola's book, to which a lot of credit is due for this book, Ricardo describes the great vocalist Caffarelli. This was back in the day of castratos. Caffarelli studied with the renowned teacher Porpora, who had Caffarelli study off of one sheet of exercises for six years. After the six years, Caffarelli said "Go forth and sing, for you are the best in Europe."

What does such an anecdote tell us about musical techniuqe? It tells us that technique is built off of a limited number of actions. And by mastering those actions, you are attaining technical mastery.

It helps to view guitar technique as a limited set of principles, with an unlimited set of applications. This book provides nine different skills to work on, all of which I consider as "baseline" skills. Skills that you will use with countless styles of music. See the character sheet below:

Name:		
Date:		
	Score	**Total Possible**
Experience Points		65660
Left Hand Coordination		6268
String Crossing		4595
Scale Technique		3387
Right Hand Coordination		2429
Slur Technique		2361
Chord Technique		929
String Skipping		581
Shifting Technique		481
Arpeggio Technique		296

In essence, you are practicing to make bricks. And you use those bricks to build buildings. In this book, you will use a core set of 20 exercises, and you will do each exercise in a variety of ways. I cannot emphasize enough the importance of using the different fingerings presented in this book. The goal of this book is to teach you how to control your hands when using the guitar. Each different fingerings will give you points in the above areas.

You gain points by performing each exercise at certain metronome settings. Once you successfully play the exercise at that given setting, you can add the points to your score card. You only add the points once, however. You must perform each fingering at each metronome level to get all of the points. I have a helpful video series that walks you through the process. Please text "Magitar1" to "44222" to receive information on registering for the series.

It is not the goal of this book to teach you to read music. It is not the goal of this book to teach you songs.

It is the goal of this book to teach you to use the guitar easily and efficiently. To teach you to push your technique, and master a few principles, all the while implementing a simple and fun point system.

I highly suggest you watch the video series that accompanies this book by texting "Magitar1" to "44222" or visiting **www.musicandguitarlessons.com/register/magitar-guitar-technique-book-1/.** I provide good, yet concise, tips and pointers as well as demonstrations of all the exercises, as well as instructions on how to track your points. Also, you can print off the character sheet found at the back of this book, so that you can start measuring your ability and progress daily.

Happy practice!

Ross Trottier
Composer, Teacher, Performer

Chapter 1

Attending the concert was risky. Sam knew it. It meant not only sneaking out on a school night, but also braving the nightlife of downtown, and getting past the doorman into the Black Emerald. Sam also knew that it would be worth it. The old guitar strapped to Sam's back would surely come home with Kyle Shreddenson's autograph.

Sam could remember the old man's face, his smile causing a cascade of wrinkles across his cheeks and down his neck. His old "box guitar". The last item at the garage sale.

"Box Guitar." That is what he had called it.

Sam was in bed by 9:30, and waited two full hours before attempting to break free for the night. At 11:29, Sam cracked the door, walked out passed the other bedrooms, carefully stepped over Rusty the basset hound, and made his way out of the house and on to bus stop number four.

The bus stop was empty, as usual. Nobody used the bus in the suburbs. Sam stood shivering in the cold, and waited calmly for the familiar sound of an approaching bus engine. Soon, he heard the buss approach and screech to a halt. The doors opened with a hiss, and Sam stepped in.

Sam flashed a bus pass to the driver, an old woman with enormous bags under her eyes. She nodded, and Sam took one of the many free seats.

A man sat in the opposite seat, and gave an oration to any that would listen. He expounded upon the virtues of the city's bus system, all the while cradling a bottle of ranch dressing in one hand like a baby. All of the other seats were empty, and the bus driver bounced in her seat not noticing.

Sam did not listen, and tried very hard not to look. Instead, the young guitarist sat, forehead resting on the cold glass, and stared at the passing street lights.

Soon, the bus screeched to a halt at stop number twenty six. Sam's stop. Sam rose, pretending not to look at the strange man, and exited the bus. Sam stepped into the noisy din of downtown, and headed for the Black Diamond.

Sam's parents would never forgive a night like this. Sam knew it, and felt the accompanying fear of being caught red handed. Drunkards lined the street, loudly goofing off in parts, sullenly smoking cigarettes in others. They all seemed to sneer, and they all seemed interested in the young guitarist.

Sam approached the Black Diamond, it's grey warehouse shape looming ahead. The sign, lit up by red neon, read "Kryborg tonight!".

Sam's heart leapt.

Below the sign, in the parking lot, mulled what must have been the entire city's rock n' roll fashion scene. They mulled about, puffing on cigarettes, running their fingers through an ocean of brightly colored hair, admiring the rips in each other's clothes, and arguing about who had the most original style.

Sam sighed.

The bouncer at the door was a literal warthog of a man. He stood tall, with a large gut protruding out, tight jeans, a wife beater, pierced septum, and a black Mohawk. He stared at Sam.

"I'm, I'm here to see Kryborg," Sam said nervously.

The warthog man snorted with laughter.

"You can't be older than thirteen! Twenty-one and up, kid. Get lost," he said.

Sam sighed, and began turning to leave.

"Aw, come on now," can a friendly voice. "Can't you remember wanting to see your favorite band at that age?" said a nearby woman. "Let the kid in."

The warthog glared at Sam, his face softened, and then moved out of the doorway.

"No alcohol, kid. Water only. Understood?" he said. The young woman laughed, and pushed Sam forward.

Sam nodded, and walked through the door into the noisy bar. The humidity inside was staggering, as was the heat. Outside it had been chilly, but inside felt like a sauna fed by sweat. The sound of the opening act was deafening, and so homogenous as to be indecipherable. Sam approached the bar.

The barkeep glared at Sam.

"Water, please," Sam said meekly.

The barkeep let out a howl of laughter, and pointed to the water fountain in the corner. Sam nodded, and walked to a lonely corner to sit. Sam could almost make the room disappear by focusing on the old box guitar.

"Are you setting up?" asked a familiar, and irritated voice.

Sam looked in shock at Kyle Shredderson.

"You're... you're..." stammered Sam.

"Kyle. And you are in my way," answered Kyle.

"I... came here to..." Sam said pointing at the old guitar.

Kyle laughed, and began inspecting the guitar.

"What a crummy old piece of junk! A sunglow? Who has ever heard of that brand?" Kyle said laughing.

Flicking the long black hair from his eyes, Kyle tossed the guitar into the crowd. The crowd yelled indignantly, until they realized who had thrown the guitar. They then commenced fighting over the guitar, rendering it into splinters.

Sam stood dumbfounded, and Kyle Shredderson began setting up smugly.

Outside, the air was cold. An improvement on the sweat box that was the black diamond. The sounds of Kyle Shredderson's guitar began to trickle out of the door. Slowly, the parking lot emptied into the Black Diamond.

Sam sat on a parking block, lip quivering.

"And what did you call that?" came a small, bossy, and semi-Irish voice.

Sam looked up to see a small bearded figure, twirling a curled moustache between thumb and finger. He held a lute with his other hand, which looked ancient and frail.

"What brand of guitar is that?" Sam asked.

The small man hooted with laughter, and sighed.

"The brand is not important my young friend.," said the small man.

"Well, don't bring it in there," Sam said bitterly, jabbing a thumb in the direction of the Black Diamond's door.

"Well, why not?" asked the small man.

"They will smash it to pieces," replied Sam.

"Ha! I would just like to see them try," said the small man defiantly.

"What, are you some sort of guitar hero? What is your name?" asked Sam.

"My name does not concern you. But I'll wager playing guitar does," said the small man.

"Why? They already broke my only guitar. And I sucked anyhow..." said Sam.

"Sucked?" asked the small man, recoiling. "Well, how long have you been playing?"

"Three weeks," answered Sam.

"Well no wonder!" laughed the man. "Your ears are green as cabbage."

The young guitarist looked indignant.

"You should play him off of the stage," said the leprechaun man.

"How? It will take me years to be as good as him," said Sam, frustrated. "I wasn't *born* being able to play like Kyle Shredderton."

"Nobody was born knowing how to play," answered the small man.

"Kyle Shredderton was," replied Sam.

"I don't know who this Shredderton is, but if you keep saying he was born knowing how to play, I am going to change your fingers into pickles. We'll see how good you play then, eh?" menaced the small man.

"And just how are you going to do that?" yelled Sam, standing up with awkwardly raised arms.

The small man snapped his finger, and Sam gave a scream. The last stragglers in the parking lot looked at Sam, then at the old man.

Where Sam once had long slender fingers, now dangled then stubby pickles, glistening with brine. Sam's arms dropped from their strange eagle pose, dripping vinegar on Sam's penny loafers.

"Change them back!" yelled Sam. "How am I going to fish these pennies out of my loafers with pickle fingers?!"

"Promise to play this Kyle character off of the stage," replied the old man, smiling.

"I don't have the time," whined Sam, arms crossed.

The small man snapped his fingers again. The parking lot froze. The smoke even ceased moving. Time had stopped.

Sam's jaws dropped, then formed into a smile as his pickle skin became human skin once again.

"You now have time," began the small man. "And I suggest you use it. A nice adventure would do you good."

The small man rubbed his chin, and twirled his moustache in thought.

"The golden string!" he exclaimed. "You will seek the golden string."

"The golden string?" asked Sam.

"Yes, the golden string. In seeking it you will become a great guitarist. Will you join me?" the small man extended his hand.

"Fine. Just no more finger pickling, ok?" replied Sam.

"Finger *picking*," said the wizard with a sly smile.

A portal opened up, and the small man led Sam by the hand.

"Where are we going?" asked Sam.

"Magitar," he replied.

Ch. 2

After stepping through the portal, Sam stood bewildered. An enchanted forest. The sky, barely visible through the foliage, was the deepest of blues. The forest glowed a sort of dark emerald, broken by bright shafts of light.

A beaten path wound its way lazily between giant hulking trees. Many enchanted life forms dashed between these monolithic pines. Faeries laughed, squirrel men chittered, electric butterflies glowed, and the enchanting sound of a plucked lute gave it all a most charming backdrop.

"Hello?!" shouted the young guitarist.

"Right here, right here," began the old man cheerily, as he stepped out from behind a blackberry bush. His lips were stained a deep purple. "How delicious these are..." he said dremily.

"I'm not hungry," returned Sam. "How did you summon that portal? Are you some sort of wizard or something?"

"Precisely," answered the wizard.

"Don't wizards have names?" asked Sam.

"Of course," answered the wizard.

"So... what is yours?" asked Sam.

"Don't ask me again. You don't know me! I am going to turn your toes into olives. The kind stuffed with cheese, if you don't quit prying," answered the wizard.

"Fine..." said the young guitarist.

"This way," beckoned the wizard, and they started off down the path through Magitar.

"Where are we going?" asked Sam.

"To my friend Arthur's house. He is the finest luthier in Magitar, and we need to see about getting you something to play," answered the wizard.

"Can't I just play your guitar?" asked Sam.

"Absolutely not!" answered the old man hotly.

"Oh... ok," stammered Sam.

Sam nodded.

"We need something that can handle the golden string. Arthur makes some of the sweetest instruments I have ever seen," continued the old wizard.

"Where is the golden string?" asked Sam.

"With the keeper," answered the wizard.

"Who is the keeper?" asked Sam.

"The one who guards the golden string," answered the wizard. "Ah, yes. Here we are."

The two broke off from the main trail, and followed a small footpath to a large yard. A beautiful cabin was situated itself in the center of this yard, with a brook tumbling just beyond the porch. Two fawns sprang away from the book at the pair's approached.

The old man began to knock on the door.

"Arthur! Arthur! It's your old friend!" yelled the wizard.

No answer.

The wizard resumed knocking on the door and shouting.

No answer.

"He's probably off looking for lumber," began the wizard. "I know him well, so let's just go in and make ourselves at home. He has tons of ice cream, and I know where he hides it."

The wizard patted his belly with one hand, and jiggled the doorknob with the other. The lock made an audible "click" and the door swung open.

Inside, the room was full of what appeared to be snakes. They slithered on the hard wood floor, creating an awful scraping noise. A man was screaming.

"Gandork!" screamed the man, all covered by the snake like creatures. He resembled a bug caught in an angry cocoon. "Gandork! Oh thank god. You mus' get these confounded things off of me!"

Sam looked over at Gandork. Gandork turned red.

"Not a word!" he yelled at Sam. "Not a word, you hear? I am from an ancient order of wizards, and my name is none of your business!"

Sam cringed at the thought of his socks smelling like olives, and looked back at the struggling man.

"Arthur," began the Wizard, "Arthur, don't fight 'em Arthur. Now what have you gone an done?"

"They are enchanted strings," said Arthur. "You know, the ones you ordered and never showed up to pay for!"

The wizard blushed for a second time.

"Oh yeah, those ones," said Gandork.

"Well, rumphf," began Arthur as the strings began to wrap their way around his mouth.

Gandork looked at Sam.

"This is an excellent time to learn how to properly pluck a string. Pluck em nice and loud! Arthur is no good to us dead," said Gandork.

Gandork began to look flustered and shook a string off of his pant leg. His shoes jingled as he shook.

Sam struck at the strings weakly.

"No!" exclaimed Gandork. "You must push the strings into motion. Not strike them. Pluck from the knuckle at the base of your hand!"

Sam plucked away, then stumbled across a pick. He picked it up and gripped with three fingers.

"No!" yelled Gandork again. "Hold the pick between your thumb and index finger, across the widest part. If you need help, take out your cell phone and text "Magitar1" to "44222" and register for the video series!"

Gandork gave Sam a thumbs up, and Sam took out a cell phone to register for the video series.

Seriously, you should register using your real cell phone.

Exercise One

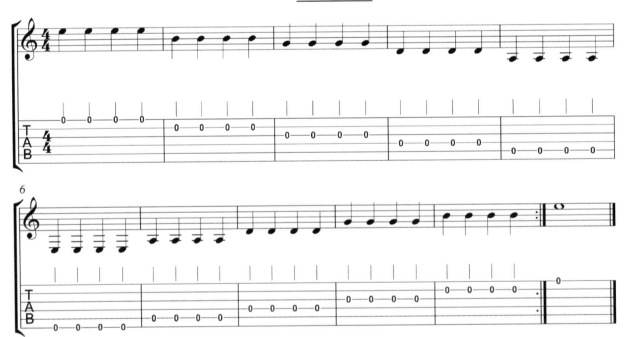

Exercise One Point Sheet

Metronome Setting	60	80	100	120	144	160	184	200
Experience Points	5	10	15	20	25	30	35	40
Right Hand Coordination	1	1	2	2	3	3	4	5
String Crossing	1	1	2	2	3	3	4	5
Fingerings								
i, i, i, i								
m, m, m, m								
a, a, a, a								
p, p, p, p								
i, m, i, m								
i, a, i, a								
m, a, m, a								
i, m, a, m								
i, a, m, a								
p, i, p, i								
p, m, p, m								
p, a, p, a								
⊓, ⊓, ⊓, ⊓								
⊓, ∨, ⊓, ∨								
∨, ∨, ∨, ∨								
⊓, ⊓, ∨, ∨								
∨, ∨, ⊓, ⊓								

	Total per Fingering	Total Possible
Experience Points	180	3060
Right Hand Coordination	21	357
String Crossing	21	357

**It is recommended that you achieve an experience point level of 100 to move forward in the adventure.

Chapter 3

Arthur couldn't stand for hours. The strings had squeezed the poor man for so long, that his legs lost circulation for many long days. Gandork whispered some words, and blew some dust into Arthur's face. Arthur sneezed and looked cross.

"Be still now," said Gandork. "Or we might have to cut off your legs."

Arthur lay back, and let out a grumble. Gandork sat and mumbled what sounded like spells for quite some time.

"Alright, right as rain, eh?" asked Gandork, smiling.

Arthur slowly stood.

"Now how about the payment," asked Arthur.

"For what?" asked Gandork.

"The what?" retorted Arthur. "The bloody enchanted strings, that's what!"

"I don't see any strings, Arthur," said Gandork.

"Well, you did when you came in!" returned Arthur.

"I also saw a luthier in above his head, begging for help," Gandork said, calmly removing a fig from his breast pocket and popping it into his mouth.

Arthur grumbled, and put a pot of water on the stove for tea.

"What'll you be needing this time?" Arthur said, defeated.

"Ahhh, it is not I that need anything this time," began Gandork. "It is Sam here who needs a proper instrument."

Arthur studied Sam.

"You are travelling with him?" he asked, pointing at Gandork.

Sam nodded.

Arthur sighed, left the room, and returned with a small case containing a plain looking guitar.

"Now, the wizard obviously has you on some sort of fool's errend," began Arthur. Gandork snorted. "So you'll be needing something that can handle some playing."

Arthur handed the guitar to Sam. Sam took it, timidly.

"Now don't be shy of it!" hollered Arthur. "I built it to last."

Gandork leapt off of the counter, brushed off his breast and announced that they would be leaving immediately.

"Thank you," Sam said earnestly, pressing Arthur's hand.

Arthur nodded.

The sun outside was bright, and Sam squinted as he slung the guitar over his shoulder. It rested against his back, secured by a thin shoelace.

"A fine day for a tune!" announced Gandork, and began whistling some discordant strange melody as they tromped down the path towards the mountains.

"To the keeper we go,

to the keeper oh!

To gather the string we go

to gather the string oh!

Stash your queens

and gather your steam

to find the string we go, oh!"

Sam tried to ignore the singing, and began to day dream about home.

The two approached a large gate, set in a large wall, set before an even larger mountain. A tall troll-like figure stood guard at the gate, wielding an enormous two handed drum stick. Next to him sat a small metal drum.

"Hear ye, hear ye! On those that beat two to my one shall pass 'ere this day," growled the troll.

Sam stared blankly.

The troll began to swing his drumstick wildly at the small metal drum, and the deepest boom echoed from the mountain behind the wall at the bottom of every strike.

"He wants you to play eighth notes!" exclaimed the wizard.

Sam continued to stare blankly.

"Look," began Gandork, plucking his string twice to every fierce beat from the troll. His rhythm was smooth and even. "Now it is your turn! If you need help, text Magitar1 to 44222 with your phone. My creator has a nifty video on the internet to show you how."

Exercise Two

Exercise Two Point Sheet

Metronome Setting	60	80	100	120	144	160	184	200
Experience Points	10	15	20	25	30	35	40	45
Right Hand Coordination	2	2	3	3	4	4	5	6
String Crossing	2	2	3	3	4	4	5	6
Fingerings								
i, i, i, i								
m, m, m, m								
a, a, a, a								
p, p, p, p								
i, m, i, m								
i, a, i, a								
m, a, m, a								
i, m, a, m								
i, a, m, a								
p, i, p, i								
p, m, p, m								
p, a, p, a								
Π, Π, Π, Π								
Π, ∨, Π, ∨								
∨, ∨, ∨, ∨								
Π, Π, ∨, ∨								
∨, ∨, Π, Π								

	Total per Fingering	Total Possible
Experience Points	220	3740
Right Hand Coordination	29	493
String Crossing	29	493

*** It is recommended that you have 200 experience points before moving forward.*

Chapter 4

The troll had beat his drum so long, that he had collapsed out of exhaustion. He lay there, his thickly muscled ribcage moving back and forth violently with his breath.

"No... more..." he panted.

"Well," announced Gandork, his hands on his hips, "you ought to let the young guitarist through, then."

"Yes... yes," began the troll. "But not you. You are not allowed back. Master says."

"Your master is a knothead! Blunder to him!" Gandork protested, pulling his lute out and preparing a chord.

The sound that filled the valley before the gates was terrifying, and the sky grew dark. Gandork was strumming so fast, his hand became a blur. He seemed to grow in stature,

"Tell me I cannot come in, Gronch! Go ahead!" Gandork yelled menacingly.

Where poor Gronch once had hair, now hung limp, grey spaghetti noodles.

The troll howled.

"Get them off of me," the troll begged. "They are all slimy!"

Gandork's eyes were daggers.

"And what about this business of not letting me through?" he asked impatiently.

The troll waved them through the gates.

The mountains on the other side of the wall were horrible to behold. Where the forest had been green, the mountains were grey, brown and a sickening black. Sam shuddered.

"Now, listen here," began Gandork. "The keeper has his goblin army in these mountains. We best keep our heads low."

"Great," Sam replied with a sigh.

The mud slurped at their shoes as they moved down the path towards the Keeper's tower. The rain began to patter in the puddles, and two figures appeared on the road ahead.

"Halt!" came a raspy, sick voice. "Who goes 'dere?"

The goblins stood in the center of the path, with the rain falling around them. Their hunched backs were visible beneath their soaked garb and their eyes squinted as if they had trouble seeing.

"Oi!" came another raspy voice. "Beggin' the questions is my job, ye hear? I'll not 'ave you barkin' orders in the presence of a distinguished officer."

"You lunkhead! It is me that has the rank 'ere!" returned the first goblin.

"Oh my!" exclaimed Gandork with a flourish. "What a pleasure to be in the presence of not one, but TWO distinguished officers in the keeper's army. May I inquire you rank?"

"I'm the captain, and this 'ere is jus' a simple footman," exclaimed the first goblin.

"Wot?! You mus' 'ave worms in yer 'ead. I'm a sergeant in the keeper's battalions, and ye best not forget it!"

"Well, well! A captain! I guess that answers the question as to who pulls rank here," replied Gandork, beaming.

"I'll show ye captain!" yelled the first goblin.

He clunked the second goblin on the top of the head with a closed fist. The second goblin fell, and began to bite the ankles of the first. The first jumped and squealed in pain, slipping in the mud. His head came down to meet the second goblin's with a loud crack. Both lay there unmoving.

Sam stared and blinked.

"Well, what are you waiting for?" asked Gandork impatiently. "Get dressed!"

After Sam and Gandork had dressed themselves in the goblin clothing, they set off down the muddy path again. The goblin shoes were made of metal, and Sam stubbed a toe with each step. Gandork looked ridiculous in the clothes, drooping down past his knees. He seemed not to mind.

Ahead came more goblin voices. Many more goblin voices.

"Uhhh, Gandork?" asked Sam.

"Yes?" returned Gandork, his lips curled in a tight smile.

"Are we going towards the goblin voices?" asked Sam.

"Why of course we are!" returned Gandork. "We have to get to the tower somehow, eh?"

As they rounded a corner, they found themselves in the midst of a goblin marching troupe. The troup lay about, eating lunch and drinking tea.

"An where 'ave you two muffons been?" asked the one in charge.

Gandork pointed behind us on the trail, his hood pulled so that his face was hidden in shadow.

"Well, we 'ave been waitin for ye! Get in line!" yelled the goblin sergeant. "I need someone to keep time, we're gonna 'ave us a march!"

The goblin looked at Sam, with the guitar slung behind his back.

"You'll do! You know the drill, low strings then high. Left then right!" yelled the goblin.

"Play the low and high strings and alternate with the sergeant! Don't lose time, these goblins might fall over if you do. Trust me, you don't want an angry troop of goblins on you in these woods. If you need help, check the video series by texting Magitar1 to 44222 with your phone. My creator will show you how," whispered Gandork hurriedly.

"Left! Right! Left! Right!" yelled the goblin sergeant as the troop moved through the rotting woods.

Exercise Three

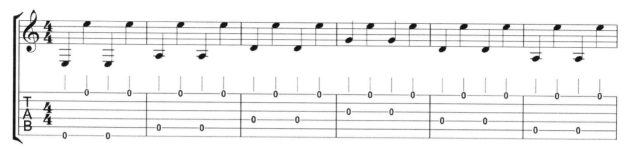

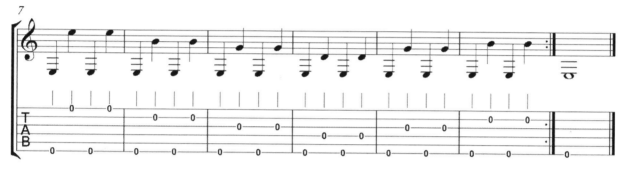

Exercise Three Point Sheet

Metronome Setting	60	80	100	120	144	160	184	200
Experience Points	5	10	15	20	25	30	35	40
Right Hand Coordination	1	1	2	2	3	3	4	5
String Skipping	1	1	2	2	3	3	4	5
Fingerings								
p, i, p, i								
p, m, p, m								
p, a, p, a								
p, i, p, m								
p, m, p, a								
p, i, p, a								
⊓, ∨, ⊓, ∨								
⊓, ⊓, ⊓, ⊓								
∨, ∨, ∨, ∨								
∨, ⊓, ∨, ⊓								

	Total per Fingering	Total Possible
Experience Points	180	1800
Right Hand Coordination	21	210
String Skipping	21	210

** It is recommended that you have 300 experience points before moving forward.

Chapter 5

They marched all day, and Sam's feet felt as if they would fall right off. The goblin sergeant called off the march after many hours, and gave orders for a fire to be started. Gandork and Sam went to find fire wood.

"This is our chance to slip off," whispered Gandork. "We will need to be quick, and make a run for it in the woods."

Sam looked nervous at this.

"Don't worry, they don't hang deserters. They lock them away in a dungeon," said Gandork reassuringly.

Sam did not look any less nervous.

Gandork ducked off under a log, and slipped away into the muddy forest. Sam followed, huffing along trying to keep up, and daydreaming of dungeons all the while.

"Quickly now!" yelled Gandork. "They won't start looking for us until nightfall, but I want to be well away before then."

The forest seemed to swallow them up. Light faded from the dense, brown foliage. Like a world endlessly subjected to a wet autumn, the forest smelled of peat and mud. Sam heard the growls and groans of various creatures, likely terrifying, and likely hostile.

"Stop," Sam panted. "I need a rest."

Gandork stopped to face Sam, and saw how earnest the young guitarist was.

"Alright," Gandork began. "But only for a few minutes."

The two sat in the dark, dank forest. The sounds around them seemed to die as two voices sounded in the distance. First, a voice high and shrill with frustration. Second, a voice low and rumbling with stubbornness.

"Do you hear that?" asked Sam.

The voices drew nearer.

"Just fellow travelers. Keep yourself quiet now," said Gandork.

Gandork pulled his garb over his body and seemed to melt into the forest. Sam attempted to do the same.

"Oi! Percy, come 'ave a look at this lil' fool troin to hid in a lil' toonik," rumbled the deep voice.

"Leave 'em alone now, Groophus. We are after the golden string, not some fool with a short cloak."

"Hey!" Sam shouted, standing. "That is the last time I let someone bully me today! Enough!"

Before Sam stood a towering ogre, and a tiny bespectacled gnome sat upon his shoulder.

"Keep moving Groophus, you knothead!" yelled the gnome.

"Oi! Now you quit pushin' on ME!" returned Groophus, the towering ogre. Drool dripped down from his overbite, and his eyes squinted with his anger. "You can't even play two notes yet, the keeper won't let you through to de string."

"Oh yeah? At least I can press the strings hard enough to even get a note in the first place!" returned Percy.

The ogre laughed.

"You press so 'ard you might jus' pop dem strings off," he yelled bellowing a laugh.

"Better than the mess you make!" returned the gnome. "You can't even make your fingers do the hinge, and you lose track of where you are all the time! How am I going to get a note if I don't push the string up to the wood?"

The gnome took out his guitar, and imitated a hinge with his index finger a pinky. His pinky lifted and placed, while the index finger stayed put. He began playing each note in succession, with extreme amounts of buzz, and it sounded out of tune. Within a few seconds, he took his hand away and shook it from fatigue.

The ogre laughed and took out his enormous guitar. He began alternating between the same two notes, his hand very relaxed and his fingers quite close to each fret. Soon, however, he lost track of where his fingers were, and had to stop.

"You are both lunkards!" shouted Gandork, appearing as if from nowhere. "You must do the hinge, as well as press lightly near the fret! That string doesn't ever touch the wood of the fingerboard. It only touches the fret."

"Wot is dis?" asked the Ogre, pointing at Gandork.

"This, this? This is a wizard," Gandork said proudly.

"Oh, good for you," began Percy. "Luckily for you, we are off to get the golden string, and Groophus here isn't partial to the taste of wizard."

"More luck for you," returned Gandork.

"You think you're better an' us?" asked Groophus, growing in anger.

"I KNOW I am better than you," returned Gandork. "So is my friend here, who is seeking the very same string."

Sam shot a nervous glance at Gandork.

"Go ahead Sam, show 'em how to do it! If you need help, use my creator's video series by texting Magitar1 to 44222," said Gandork.

Exercise Four

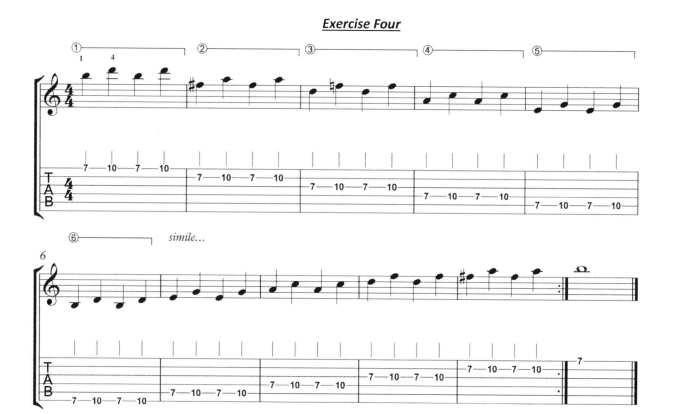

Exercise Four Point Sheet

Metronome Setting	60	80	100	120	144	160	184	200
Experience Points	10	15	20	25	30	35	40	45
Left Hand Coordination	2	2	3	3	4	4	5	6
String Crossing	2	2	3	3	4	4	5	6
Scale Technique	1	1	2	2	3	3	4	5
Fingerings								
i, m, i, m								
i, a, i, a								
m, a, m, a								
i, m, a, m								
i, a, m, a								
p, i, p, i								
p, m, p, m								
p, a, p, a								
⊓, ⊓, ⊓, ⊓								
⊓, ∨, ⊓, ∨								
∨, ∨, ∨, ∨								
⊓, ⊓, ∨, ∨								
∨, ∨, ⊓, ⊓								

	Total per Fingering	Total Possible
Experience Points	220	2860
Left Hand Coordination	29	377
String Crossing	29	377
Scale Technique	21	273

*** It is recommended that you have 400 experience points before moving forward.*

Exercise Five

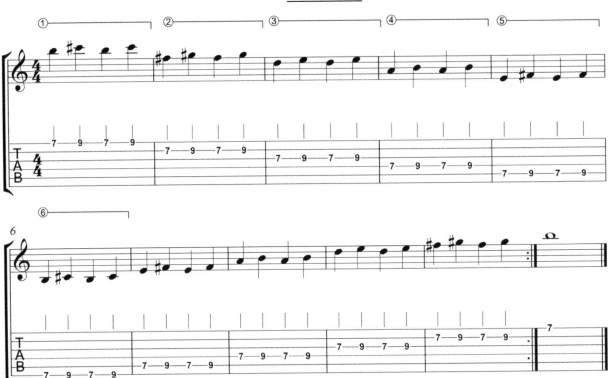

Exercise Five Point Sheet

Metronome Setting	60	80	100	120	144	160	184	200
Experience Points	10	15	20	25	30	35	40	45
Left Hand Coordination	2	2	3	3	4	4	5	6
String Crossing	2	2	3	3	4	4	5	6
Scale Technique	1	1	2	2	3	3	4	5
Fingerings								
i, m, i, m								
i, a, i, a								
m, a, m, a								
i, m, a, m								
i, a, m, a								
p, i, p, i								
p, m, p, m								
p, a, p, a								
Π, Π, Π, Π								
Π, ⋁, Π, ⋁								
⋁, ⋁, ⋁, ⋁								
Π, Π, ⋁, ⋁								
⋁, ⋁, Π, Π								

	Total per Fingering	Total Possible
Experience Points	220	2860
Left Hand Coordination	29	377
String Crossing	29	377
Scale Technique	21	273

** It is recommended that you have 500 experience points before moving forward.

Exercise Six

Exercise Six Point Sheet

Metronome Setting	60	80	100	120	144	160	184	200
Experience Points	10	15	20	25	30	35	40	45
Left Hand Coordination	2	2	3	3	4	4	5	6
String Crossing	2	2	3	3	4	4	5	6
Scale Technique	1	1	2	2	3	3	4	5
Fingerings								
i, m, i, m								
i, a, i, a								
m, a, m, a								
i, m, a, m								
i, a, m, a								
p, i, p, i								
p, m, p, m								
p, a, p, a								
Π, Π, Π, Π								
Π, V, Π, V								
V, V, V, V								
Π, Π, V, V								
V, V, Π, Π								

	Total per Fingering	Total Possible
Experience Points	220	2860
Left Hand Coordination	29	377
String Crossing	29	377
Scale Technique	21	273

** It is recommended that you have 600 experience points before moving forward.

Exercise Seven

Exercise Seven Point Sheet

Metronome Setting	60	80	100	120	144	160	184	200
Experience Points	15	20	25	30	35	40	45	50
Left Hand Coordination	3	3	4	4	5	5	6	7
String Crossing	3	3	4	4	5	5	6	7
Scale Technique	2	2	3	3	4	4	5	6
Fingerings								
i, m, i, m								
i, a, i, a								
m, a, m, a								
i, m, a, m								
i, a, m, a								
p, i, p, i								
p, m, p, m								
p, a, p, a								
П, П, П, П								
П, V, П, V								
V, V, V, V								
П, П, V, V								
V, V, П, П								

	Total per Fingering	Total Possible
Experience Points	260	3380
Left Hand Coordination	37	481
String Crossing	37	481
Scale Technique	29	377

** It is recommended that you have 700 experience points before moving forward.

Exercise Eight

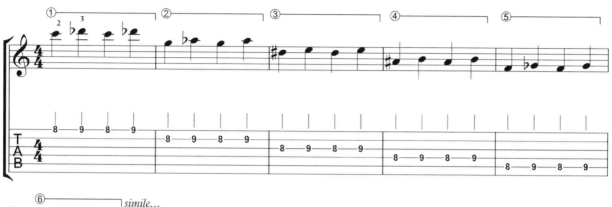

Exercise Eight Point Sheet

Metronome Setting	60	80	100	120	144	160	184	200
Experience Points	15	20	25	30	35	40	45	50
Left Hand Coordination	3	3	4	4	5	5	6	7
String Crossing	3	3	4	4	5	5	6	7
Scale Technique	2	2	3	3	4	4	5	6
Fingerings								
i, m, i, m								
i, a, i, a								
m, a, m, a								
i, m, a, m								
i, a, m, a								
p, i, p, i								
p, m, p, m								
p, a, p, a								
Π, Π, Π, Π								
Π, ∨, Π, ∨								
∨, ∨, ∨, ∨								
Π, Π, ∨, ∨								
∨, ∨, Π, Π								

	Total per Fingering	Total Possible
Experience Points	260	3380
Left Hand Coordination	37	481
String Crossing	37	481
Scale Technique	29	377

** It is recommended that you have 800 experience points before moving forward.

Exercise Nine

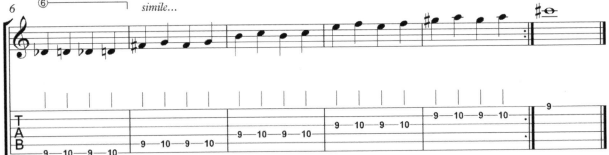

Exercise Nine Point Sheet

Metronome Setting	60	80	100	120	144	160	184	200
Experience Points	15	20	25	30	35	40	45	50
Left Hand Coordination	3	3	4	4	5	5	6	7
String Crossing	3	3	4	4	5	5	6	7
Scale Technique	2	2	3	3	4	4	5	6
Fingerings								
i, m, i, m								
i, a, i, a								
m, a, m, a								
i, m, a, m								
i, a, m, a								
p, i, p, i								
p, m, p, m								
p, a, p, a								
П, П, П, П								
П, ᵛ, П, ᵛ								
ᵛ, ᵛ, ᵛ, ᵛ								
П, П, ᵛ, ᵛ								
ᵛ, ᵛ, П, П								

	Total per Fingering	Total Possible
Experience Points	260	3380
Left Hand Coordination	37	481
String Crossing	37	481
Scale Technique	29	377

** *It is recommended that you have 900 experience points before moving forward.*

Chapter 6

Percy and Groophus gawked at Sam. Those fingers moved so fast and light. It was certainly not fair

"Dis is wut I get fer listening to you!" yelled Groophus angrily.

"No surprise there, Groophus not thinking for himself. Hrumpf!" returned Percy in his shrill voice.

"Oi! I let you roide my shoulders all the way from de plains to Magitar!" yelled Groophus.

"And what good it did me!" yelled Percy, dropping to the ground. He landed lightly on his feet and dashed off into the forest.

Groophus' lower lip quivered with hurt and his eyes welled with tears. He stood, and began bumbling after the little gnome. The forest rang with his cries of regret.

Gandork slapped Sam on the shoulder and smiled. They continued through the wood until they came upon a large black road. Its shiny surface snaked through the woods, carving a path through the mists.

"The keeper's road," said Gandork with a smile.

"I don't like it," said Sam.

Gandork's smile widened as they continued down the sulky road. Before much time passed, the road began to branch off in odd directions, sometimes looping back upon itself, sometimes wandering for miles.

Sam felt exhausted.

"Do you know the way?" Sam asked.

"That, my friend, I do not," replied Gandork.

Sam stopped, and glared at Gandork. Gandork glared back.

"Well," Gandork said irritiably. "I do, in a way, know. You see, there are strange creatures that travel this world. They sing strange melodies, and guide travelers that can join in their macabre tune. It's mostly chromatic really, with a few odd whole steps in there. Luckily," he said gleefully, "it plays very well on the guitar."

"Chromatic?" asked Sam.

Gandork reached into his bag and pulled out a dusty old volume. "Music Theory in One Lesson," it said across the cover.

"One day, I hope you will read this," said Gandork. "You will learn that and much more. But, alas! This adventure is about learning how to touch the guitar properly. Technique, Sam. But, if you want to know more, you can check out the music theory video series at my creator's website."

Gandork smiled.

"Well, how do you play it?" asked Sam.

Exercise Ten

Exercise Ten Point Sheet

Metronome Setting	60	80	100	120	144	160	184	200
Experience Points	20	25	30	35	40	45	50	55
Left Hand Coordination	4	4	5	5	6	6	7	8
String Crossing	3	3	4	4	5	5	6	7
Scale Technique	4	4	5	5	6	6	7	8
Fingerings								
i, m, i, m								
i, a, i, a								
m, a, m, a								
i, m, a, m								
i, a, m, a								
p, i, p, i								
p, m, p, m								
p, a, p, a								
⊓, ⊓, ⊓, ⊓								
⊓, ∨, ⊓, ∨								
∨, ∨, ∨, ∨								
⊓, ⊓, ∨, ∨								
∨, ∨, ⊓, ⊓								

	Total per Fingering	Total Possible
Experience Points	300	3900
Left Hand Coordination	45	585
String Crossing	37	481
Scale Technique	45	585

** It is recommended that you have 1000 experience points before moving forward.

Sam played and played. At first, the melody was slow. He had trouble speeding it up. The notes would buzz.

"Keep each finger down as you place the next!" hollered Gandork. "Lift them all at once when you cross to the next string."

Sam's forehead began to bead sweat.

"Closer to the frets!" sang Gandork, doing a jig. "Right behind 'em! Like you can feel em."

Soon, Sam's notes were clearer. Faster. And as that macabre melody took shape, so did the great shadows. They beckoned, doing a sort of dance no human could do. Their bodies had no joints, but they flowed over the black road as if made from the very same fabric.

Gandork followed. Sam followed. The shadows led through the maze of dark, shining road.

A large dark spire loomed ahead of them. The keeper's castle. Soon, what had been a thin needle extending upward into the misty sky, was now an enormous tower many hundreds of feet in diameter. The gates were of heavy ebony, shining with what light was able to penetrate the foggy skies.

The gates were now, suddenly, very close. The shadows dissipated, as did Sam's playing. The large black doors seemed impossible to move, such was their weight. Inlaid in the door was a sound hole, over which strings were strung.

Many hundreds of strings. Some so thick, it would be impossible to imagine the sort of creature that could pluck it.

Sam examined the strings as Gandork strode up to the doors, plucking each string as he passed it, listening attentively.

"Here they are!" exclaimed Gandork.

Sam looked at Gandork quizzically.

"E, A, D, G, B, E! All of them here. Just like on your guitar! Don't bother trying those thicker strings, you won't be able to budge them. Those are for the giants," Gandork said with a smile. "They are tuned so low, that you wouldn't even be able to hear the notes!"

Sam walked up to the strings, and plucked a few. Then he waited.

No answer.

"The butler," Gandork began, wringing his hands, "he is a bit hard of, eh, hearing. You'll have to try to pluck two strings at once if you want him to hear you."

Exercise Eleven

Exercise Eleven Point Sheet

Metronome Setting	60	80	100	120	144	160	184	200
Experience Points	10	15	20	25	30	35	40	45
Right Hand Coordination	2	2	3	3	4	4	5	6
String Crossing	1	1	2	2	3	3	4	5
Chord Technique	1	1	2	2	3	3	4	5
Fingerings								
p i, p i, p i, p i								
p m, p m, p m, p m								
p a, p a, p a, p a								
i m, i m, i m, i m								
i a, i a, i a, i a								
m a, m a, m a, m a								
p i, p m, p a, p m								
i m, i a, m a, i a								
п, п, п, п								
п, v, п, v								
v, v, v, v								
п, п, v, v								
v, v, п, п								

	Total per Fingering	Total Possible
Experience Points	220	2860
Right Hand Coordination	29	377
String Crossing	21	273
Chord Technique	21	273

** It is recommended that you have 1100 experience points before moving forward.

Still no answer.

"Ok," said Gandork. "Three! He must really be getting old."

Exercise Twelve

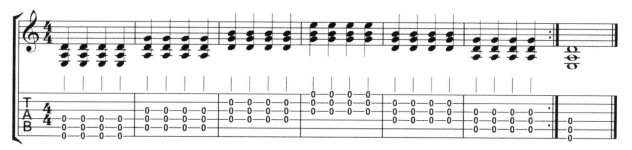

Exercise Twelve Point Sheet

Metronome Setting	60	80	100	120	144	160	184	200
Experience Points	15	20	25	30	35	40	45	50
RIght Hand Coordination	3	3	4	4	5	5	6	7
String Crossing	1	1	2	2	3	3	4	5
Chord Technique	2	2	3	3	4	4	5	6
Fingerings								
p i m , p i m , p i m								
i m a , i m a , i m a								
Π, Π, Π, Π								
Π, Ѵ, Π, Ѵ								
Ѵ, Ѵ, Ѵ, Ѵ								
Π, Π, Ѵ, Ѵ								
Ѵ, Ѵ, Π, Π								

	Total per Fingering	Total Possible
Experience Points	260	1820
RIght Hand Coordination	37	259
String Crossing	21	147
Chord Technique	29	203

*** It is recommended that you have 1200 experience points before moving forward.*

Still, no answer.

"Ok! Four!" commanded Gandork.

Exercise Thirteen

Exercise Thirteen Point Sheet

Metronome Setting	60	80	100	120	144	160	184	200
Experience Points	20	25	30	35	40	45	50	55
Right Hand Coordination	4	4	5	5	6	6	7	8
String Crossing	1	1	2	2	3	3	4	5
Chord Technique	3	3	4	4	5	5	6	7
Fingerings								
p i m a , p i m a								
Π, Π, Π, Π								
Π, V, Π, V								
V, V, V, V								
Π, Π, V, V								
V, V, Π, Π								

	Total per Fingering	Total Possible
Experience Points	300	1800
Right Hand Coordination	45	270
String Crossing	21	126
Chord Technique	37	222

*** It is recommended that you have 1300 experience points before moving forward.*

Again. No answer.

"Ok," said Gandork. "Let the infernal racket begin! Give 'em all six," said Gandork gravely, bringing his hands to his ears like ear muffs.

Exercise Fourteen

Metronome Setting	60	80	100	120	144	160	184	200
Experience Points	10	15	20	25	30	35	40	45
Right Hand Coordination	1	1	2	2	3	3	4	5
String Crossing	1	1	2	2	3	3	4	5
Chord Technique	1	1	2	2	3	3	4	5

Fingerings								
p i m a , p i m a								
RAS: i, e, a, m								
i, i, i, i*								
m, m, m, m*								
a, a, a, a*								
p, p, p, p*								
Π, Π, Π, Π								
Π, ˅, Π, ˅								
˅, ˅, ˅, ˅								
Π, Π, ˅, ˅								
˅, ˅, Π, Π								

**Alternate up and down strokes using fingers.*

	Total per Fingering	Total Possible
Experience Points	220	2420
Right Hand Coordination	21	231
String Crossing	21	231
Chord Technique	21	231

*** It is recommended that you have 1400 experience points before moving forward.*

The cacophony was startling, and Sam's ears began to ring. As the last of the notes began to fade, Sam heard a soft creak from the door. A small man, with enormous ears, a wide yet empty smile, stepped out.

"You called?" he asked.

"We are here for the golden string," said Gandork.

"All who quesht for the schtring are welcome, you muscht know," the small butler began, making slurping noises as he talked. "You muscht pass the trials to confront the keeper."

"We will pass the trials," said Gandork gravely.

The butler looked at Sam.

"And you?" he asked.

"I will pass the trials," said Sam, brandishing a guitar.

The butler bowed, and the two entered the tower.

Chapter 7

Inside, there seemed to be two things and two things only. Guitars, and strangeness. Doors, which looked like walls, strings strung about everywhere, stairs set upside down into the roof, and green flames spurting from various holes in the masonry.

The butler sat down on a chair, upholstered with red velvet, and promptly went to sleep. He looked almost like a small doll, laying limply on the seat cushion. Gandork beckoned for Sam to follow, and the two approached an elevator-like contraption that extended into the upper reaches of the tower. They entered.

Inside, where Sam was accustomed to seeing elevator buttons, was another inlaid sound hole with strings. This one, however, was much smaller. It was, in fact, the very same size as Sam's guitar.

"You must speak the tower's language," Gandork began. "Much like we did with the shadows. This elevator speaks in arpeggios. Rising arpeggios."

"What are arpeggios?" asked Sam.

"They come in many forms," began Gandork. "But the kind we need today are the kind that cross strings. You will want to make the strings ring together. My master can show you if you watch the video series."

Sam nodded.

Exercise Fifteen

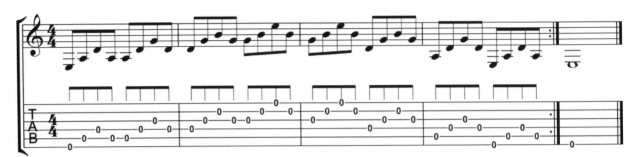

Exercise Fifteen Point Sheet

Metronome Setting	60	80	100	120	144	160	184	200
Experience Points	15	20	25	30	35	40	45	50
Right Hand Coordination	2	2	3	3	4	4	5	6
String Crossing	3	3	4	4	5	5	6	7
Arpeggio Technique	3	3	4	4	5	5	6	7
Fingerings								
p, i, m, i								
p, i, a, i								
i, m, a, m								
p, m, a, m								
Π, Π, V, V								
Π, V, Π, V								
V, Π, V, Π								
Π, Π, Π, V								

	Total per Fingering	Total Possible
Experience Points	260	2080
Right Hand Coordination	29	232
String Crossing	37	296
Arpeggio Technique	37	296

** It is recommended that you have 1500 experience points before moving forward.

Sam's arpeggios began to build with speed and smoothness over time, and the elevator began to ascend the tall dark cement tube.

"That's it!" yelled Gandork excitedly. "Keep going!"

Sam played and played, and at last the elevator stopped and they both stepped out onto a high platform.

"Now, we must play some more chromatic stuff," said Gandork. "Don't worry, the shadows won't hear this time. Play across the string, and tell the tower to move this platform across to the keeper's door! Don't forget to watch the video series for some great tips!"

Exercise Sixteen

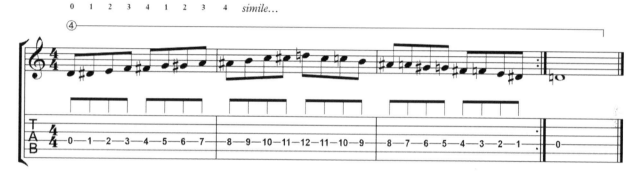

Exercise Sixteen Point Sheet

Metronome Setting	60	80	100	120	144	160	184	200
Experience Points	15	20	25	30	35	40	45	50
Left Hand Coordination	2	2	3	3	4	4	5	6
Scale Technique	3	3	4	4	5	5	6	7
Shifting Technique	3	3	4	4	5	5	6	7
Fingerings								
i, m, i, m								
i, a, i, a								
m, a, m, a								
i, m, a, m								
i, a, m, a								
p, i, p, i								
p, m, p, m								
p, a, p, a								
∏, ∏, ∏, ∏								
∏, ∨, ∏, ∨								
∨, ∨, ∨, ∨								
∏, ∏, ∨, ∨								
∨, ∨, ∏, ∏								

	Total per Fingering	Total Possible
Experience Points	260	3380
Left Hand Coordination	29	377
Scale Technique	37	481
Shifting Technique	37	481

** It is recommended that you have 1600 experience points before moving forward.

The platform moved across, and Sam was frightened by the vast fall beneath them.

"Don't worry," said Gandork. "This platform hasn't fallen in thousands of years."

They stepped off onto a landing, with another heavy door. This one, however, was different. There was a sound-hole, and strings strung over it. But this sound-hole was carved into a part of the door that curved outward. Where the door ended, and fingerboard jutted out.

Sam reached for the strings to pluck them, but could never seem to reach them.

"They are charmed," said Gandork. "You will have to use your left hand only, and pluck them over the fingerboard."

Exercise 17

**** It is highly recommended that you watch the video example for this exercise*****

Exercise 17 Point Sheet

Metronome Setting	60	80	100	120	144	160	184	200
Experience Points	15	20	25	30	35	40	45	50
Left Hand Coordination	3	3	4	4	5	5	6	7
Slur Technique	3	3	4	4	5	5	6	7
Fingerings								
1, 2, 3, 4								
1, 2, 4, 3								
1, 3, 2, 4								
1, 3, 4, 2								
1, 4, 2, 3								
1, 4, 3, 2								
2, 1, 3, 4								
2, 1, 4, 3								
2, 3, 1, 4								
2, 3, 4, 1								
2, 4, 3, 1								
2, 4, 1, 3								
3, 1, 2, 4								
3, 1, 4, 2								
3, 2, 1, 4								
3, 2, 4, 1								
3, 4, 1, 2								
3, 4, 2, 1								
4, 1, 2, 3								
4, 1, 3, 2								
4, 2, 1, 3								
4, 2, 3, 1								
4, 3, 2, 1								
4, 3, 1, 2								

** It is recommended that you have 1700 experience points before moving forward.

	Total per Fingering	Total Possible
Experience Points	260	6240
Left Hand Coordination	37	888
Slur Technique	37	888

No answer.

"Ugh!" said Gandork, wringing his hands. "Don't tell me the bloody keeper is hard at hearing these days too!"

Sam sighed.

"Let's just do all six," said Gandork, covering his ears.

Exercise 18

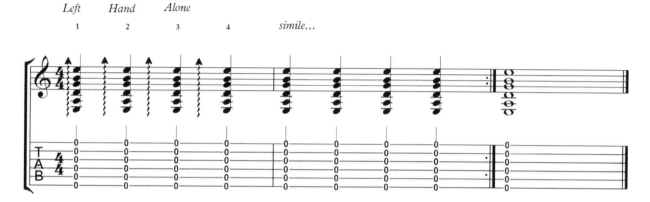

Exercise 18 Point Sheet

Metronome Setting	60	80	100	120	144	160	184	200
Experience Points	15	20	25	30	35	40	45	50
Left Hand Coordination	3	3	4	4	5	5	6	7
Slur Technique	3	3	4	4	5	5	6	7

Fingerings								
1, 2, 3, 4								
1, 2, 4, 3								
1, 3, 2, 4								
1, 3, 4, 2								
1, 4, 2, 3								
1, 4, 3, 2								
2, 1, 3, 4								
2, 1, 4, 3								
2, 3, 1, 4								
2, 3, 4, 1								
2, 4, 3, 1								
2, 4, 1, 3								
3, 1, 2, 4								
3, 1, 4, 2								
3, 2, 1, 4								
3, 2, 4, 1								
3, 4, 1, 2								
3, 4, 2, 1								
4, 1, 2, 3								
4, 1, 3, 2								
4, 2, 1, 3								
4, 2, 3, 1								
4, 3, 2, 1								
4, 3, 1, 2								

	Total per Fingering	Total Possible
Experience Points	260	6240
Left Hand Coordination	37	888
Slur Technique	37	888

** It is recommended that you have 1800 experience points before moving forward.

The door began to shake and rumble, and a large knight clad in black armor flung open the passage into his quarters. He was howling and bellowing.

"Who disturbs me?!" came a loud voice, angry and surprised.

"It is I!" chirped Gandork. "And I have another who seeks the golden string."

"Not you again, Gandork," the knight said. "Have I not told you to call before you just show up, trying for my string again."

"Again?" asked Sam. "What happened to the last kid?"

"Erm..." Gandork began to squirm.

"Let's get this over with," the Keeper said with a sigh.

Upon entering the room, Sam saw many guitars both hanging on the walls as well as built right into the tower. A golden string lit the entire chamber, and large amplifiers stood stacked in the center.

Flame erupted from the Keeper's helmet, and he began head banging in incessantly on top of the amplifiers as they rang with heavily distorted notes. The Keeper looked down at Sam, and began to play his guitar with his left hand only.

"He wants you to match him!" yelled Gandork. "Do hammer on's and pull off's! Remember, my creator has some cool videos you can access by texting XXXXXX to XXXXXXXXXX, if you need some good pointers."

Sam brandished the old guitar, and began.

Exercise 19

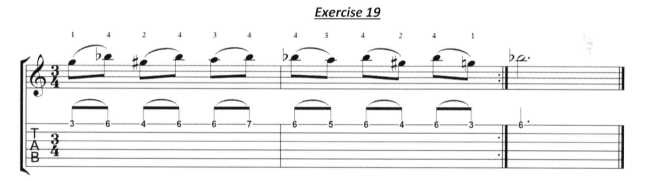

Exercise 19 Point Sheet

Metronome Setting	60	80	100	120	144	160	184	200
Experience Points	30	35	40	45	50	55	60	65
Left Hand Coordination	4	4	5	5	6	6	7	8
Slur Technique	4	4	5	5	6	6	7	8
Fingerings								
i, m, i, m								
i, a, i, a								
m, a, m, a								
i, m, a, m								
i, a, m, a								
p, i, p, i								
p, m, p, m								
p, a, p, a								
П, П, П, П								
П, ᵛ, П, ᵛ								
ᵛ, ᵛ, ᵛ, ᵛ								
П, П, ᵛ, ᵛ								
ᵛ, ᵛ, П, П								

	Total per Fingering	Total Possible
Experience Points	380	4940
Left Hand Coordination	45	585
Slur Technique	45	585

** It is recommended that you have 1900 experience points before moving forward.

The Keeper howled in frustration, and began to summon fire all around the trio of figures next to the amplifiers.

"Quick! Summon the shadows! You will need a louder, more dissonant melody for them to hear us in here, but they will do just the trick," said Gandork. "Chromatic Octaves! Yes! Check out the videos if you need help with this one, it is tricky!"

Exercise 20

Exercise 20 Point Sheet

Metronome Setting	60	80	100	120	144	160	184	200
Experience Points	30	35	40	45	50	55	60	65
Left Hand Coordination	5	5	6	6	7	7	8	9
String Skipping	5	5	6	6	7	7	8	9
String Crossing	5	5	6	6	7	7	8	9
Scale Technique	5	5	6	6	7	7	8	9
Fingerings								
p, i, m, p								
p, m, a, p								
p, i, a, p								
p, m, a, i								
⊓, ⋁, ⊓, ⋁								
⊓, ⊓, ⋁, ⋁								
⋁, ⋁, ⊓, ⊓								

	Total per Fingering	Total Possible
Experience Points	380	2660
Left Hand Coordination	53	371
String Skipping	53	371
String Crossing	53	371
Scale Technique	53	371

** It is recommended that you have 5000 experience points before moving forward to the next book.

The shadows emerged, all dancing to the strange chromatic melody that floated about the cavern. Their presence brought a sort of chill, and the fires went out as if a gust of wind were extinguishing a candle. The slender bodies of the shadows moved towards the Keeper, and twisted about his limbs, embracing him in a strange dance.

The poor Knight's armor creaked and groaned as he was forced to dance. The shadows continued as Sam's notes urged them forward.

"What sssssshould we do with him masssssterrr?" one of them asked, with a strange drawl.

Gandork looked at Sam gravely. Sam moved towards the golden string.

"You have sought the golden string, and in so seeking you have set yourself on a path to become a great guitarist. You do not need that string."

Sam looked confused.

"The string is just spraypainted gold. The keeper here is really the big dork. It is in seeking the string that you have gained your wisdom and ability," Gandork continued. "Now, what will you do with the Keeper?"

TO BE CONTINUED IN THE NEXT BOOK

CHOICE 1 - Join the Keeper and travel to the underworld to shred metal guitar.

CHOICE 2 - Bring the Keeper to the world of clouds, to save his soul and serenade him with classical guitar.

CHOICE 3 - Bring the Keeper to purgatory, and sing some sorrowful blues.

CHOICE 4 - Bring the Keeper to Gandork's magical Ireland to pluck folk tunes.

Use the character sheets in the following pages to continue to track your experience points.

Name:		
Date:		
	Score	**Total Possible**
Experience Points		65660
Left Hand Coordination		6268
String Crossing		4595
Scale Technique		3387
Right Hand Coordination		2429
Slur Technique		2361
Chord Technique		929
String Skipping		581
Shifting Technique		481
Arpeggio Technique		296

Name:		
Date:		
	Score	**Total Possible**
Experience Points		65660
Left Hand Coordination		6268
String Crossing		4595
Scale Technique		3387
Right Hand Coordination		2429
Slur Technique		2361
Chord Technique		929
String Skipping		581
Shifting Technique		481
Arpeggio Technique		296

Name:		
Date:		
	Score	**Total Possible**
Experience Points		65660
Left Hand Coordination		6268
String Crossing		4595
Scale Technique		3387
Right Hand Coordination		2429
Slur Technique		2361
Chord Technique		929
String Skipping		581
Shifting Technique		481
Arpeggio Technique		296

Name:		
Date:		
	Score	**Total Possible**
Experience Points		65660
Left Hand Coordination		6268
String Crossing		4595
Scale Technique		3387
Right Hand Coordination		2429
Slur Technique		2361
Chord Technique		929
String Skipping		581
Shifting Technique		481
Arpeggio Technique		296

	Score	Total Possible
Name:		
Date:		
Experience Points		65660
Left Hand Coordination		6268
String Crossing		4595
Scale Technique		3387
Right Hand Coordination		2429
Slur Technique		2361
Chord Technique		929
String Skipping		581
Shifting Technique		481
Arpeggio Technique		296

		Score	Total Possible
Name:			
Date:			
Experience Points			65660
Left Hand Coordination			6268
String Crossing			4595
Scale Technique			3387
Right Hand Coordination			2429
Slur Technique			2361
Chord Technique			929
String Skipping			581
Shifting Technique			481
Arpeggio Technique			296

	Score	Total Possible
Name:		
Date:		
Experience Points		65660
Left Hand Coordination		6268
String Crossing		4595
Scale Technique		3387
Right Hand Coordination		2429
Slur Technique		2361
Chord Technique		929
String Skipping		581
Shifting Technique		481
Arpeggio Technique		296

Name:		
Date:		
	Score	**Total Possible**
Experience Points		65660
Left Hand Coordination		6268
String Crossing		4595
Scale Technique		3387
Right Hand Coordination		2429
Slur Technique		2361
Chord Technique		929
String Skipping		581
Shifting Technique		481
Arpeggio Technique		296

Name:		
Date:		
	Score	**Total Possible**
Experience Points		65660
Left Hand Coordination		6268
String Crossing		4595
Scale Technique		3387
Right Hand Coordination		2429
Slur Technique		2361
Chord Technique		929
String Skipping		581
Shifting Technique		481
Arpeggio Technique		296

	Score	Total Possible
Name:		
Date:		
Experience Points		65660
Left Hand Coordination		6268
String Crossing		4595
Scale Technique		3387
Right Hand Coordination		2429
Slur Technique		2361
Chord Technique		929
String Skipping		581
Shifting Technique		481
Arpeggio Technique		296

	Score	Total Possible
Name:		
Date:		
Experience Points		65660
Left Hand Coordination		6268
String Crossing		4595
Scale Technique		3387
Right Hand Coordination		2429
Slur Technique		2361
Chord Technique		929
String Skipping		581
Shifting Technique		481
Arpeggio Technique		296

Name:		
Date:		
	Score	**Total Possible**
Experience Points		65660
Left Hand Coordination		6268
String Crossing		4595
Scale Technique		3387
Right Hand Coordination		2429
Slur Technique		2361
Chord Technique		929
String Skipping		581
Shifting Technique		481
Arpeggio Technique		296

		Score	Total Possible
Name:			
Date:			
Experience Points			65660
Left Hand Coordination			6268
String Crossing			4595
Scale Technique			3387
Right Hand Coordination			2429
Slur Technique			2361
Chord Technique			929
String Skipping			581
Shifting Technique			481
Arpeggio Technique			296

	Score	Total Possible
Name:		
Date:		
Experience Points		65660
Left Hand Coordination		6268
String Crossing		4595
Scale Technique		3387
Right Hand Coordination		2429
Slur Technique		2361
Chord Technique		929
String Skipping		581
Shifting Technique		481
Arpeggio Technique		296

	Score	Total Possible
Name:		
Date:		
Experience Points		65660
Left Hand Coordination		6268
String Crossing		4595
Scale Technique		3387
Right Hand Coordination		2429
Slur Technique		2361
Chord Technique		929
String Skipping		581
Shifting Technique		481
Arpeggio Technique		296

	Score	Total Possible
Name:		
Date:		
Experience Points		65660
Left Hand Coordination		6268
String Crossing		4595
Scale Technique		3387
Right Hand Coordination		2429
Slur Technique		2361
Chord Technique		929
String Skipping		581
Shifting Technique		481
Arpeggio Technique		296

74533901R00040

Made in the USA
Middletown, DE
26 May 2018